GOODBYE TO BEDTIME FEARS PARENTS' GUIDE

The Challenge of Putting a Frightened Child to Bed

SHERRY HENIG, Ph. D.

Brenner Publishing, LLC
Plainview, New York

Copyright © 2011. Sherry Henig, Ph.D.

This publication is designed to provide information with regard to the subject matter covered. It is written with the understanding that the author is not engaged in rendering psychological services. If expert assistance is needed, the services of a competent professional should be sought.

Brenner Publishing, LLC
516-433-0804
www.BrennerPublishing.com
www.SherryHenig.com

ISBN13: 978-0-9777203-6-1
Library of Congress Control Number: 2011933125

Printed in the United States of America
10   9   8   7   6   5   4   3   2   1

The Bedtime Experience

Bedtime can provide some of the sweetest of moments for you and your child. Confiding the highlights of the day, reading favorite books and sharing cuddles and kisses can all make for a very special time.

But bedtime can also be the source of some of the most upsetting interactions for you and your child. She may resist having her day come to an end. Having to stop playing and put away her toys, or stop being entertained by the television or the computer, or stop spending time with Mom or Dad is not appealing. Therefore, your child may fuss when she is told to prepare for bedtime. The fuss can easily turn into a battle. And the bedtime can drag on for minutes, if not hours, resulting in everyone behaving angrily towards one another and everyone feeling tired and grouchy the next day.

Sleep Problems in Children

If you and your child are having bedtime stress, you're not alone. Indeed, sleep problems are so common in young children that they actually have a formal diagnosis: "behavioral insomnia of childhood," or BIC for short. There are three types of BIC, and their technical terms are sleep-onset association type, limit-setting type, and combined type.

The sleep-onset association type is when a child's bedtime struggles and middle of the night struggles occur because she wants a specific item (like a favorite stuffed animal) or person (usually her parent) with whom to fall asleep.

The limit-setting type is when a child doesn't mind going to sleep on her own, she just doesn't want to.

This type of problem involves parents who have trouble creating and implementing rules about bedtime, thus setting the stage for their child to try to get his way by stalling or refusing to go to bed.

The combined type is when the child procrastinates bedtime while her parents are tearing their hair out trying to get her in bed, and, once there, she is unable to stay in her bedroom alone unless everything she wants is there, and this usually means one of her exhausted parents.

Bedtime Fears

Pretend Fears

Just as there are different types of children's sleep problems, there are different types of bedtime fears. There are "fears" and there are fears. The "fears" type applies to a situation in which the child says she is afraid, but she is really not afraid at all, she just does not want to go to bed. She is able to be in her bedroom alone and can fall asleep alone, but she would rather stay up and hang out. This is related to the *limit-setting type* of sleep problem, and the child's use of the "fear" word happens to be her strategy to stall bedtime. A child's procrastination at bedtime is sometimes labeled "bedtime resistance," and the problem in which a child refuses to go to bed altogether is sometimes called "bedtime refusal."

The Sleep Fairy, a book written by Janie Peterson, is a wonderful tool for parents to use with bedtime resisters and refusers. *The Sleep Fairy* is a colorful children's picture book that includes a short tear-out guide for parents. The book tells the story of Molly and Katie, two little bedtime resisters, who agitate their parents with repeated requests for attention after they are put to bed. The children then have an opportunity to read a "magical story" about a sleep fairy who watches over children in the evening. If children stay in their beds, and are very still and quiet, the sleep fairy places a gift under their pillows (much like the tooth fairy.) The children in the story test out the possibility of getting a visit from the sleep fairy by staying in their beds, after having been put to bed by their parents. The next morning they find a small gift from the sleep fairy.

Children reading this book may be motivated to go to bed, and stay in their beds, if they feel that they, too, may get a visit from the sleep fairy. Of course, in order for this enchanting book to work, a child's parents need to leave a little reward or prize under their child's pillow – but *only* if the child adheres to the bedtime routine that has been laid out for them. Peterson's parent guide helps the parent learn the subtleties of how to carry out this plan successfully and how to wean a child off the book (and the associated rewards) as he learns to fall asleep in his own bed. This method is often mistaken for bribery by some parents; however, bribery is used prior to a behavior, and this program strictly advises parents to reward their child only *after* she has performed the desired behavior.

Real Fears

Unlike bedtime resisters, many children describe bedtime concerns that truly frighten them. Sometimes these fears are associated with problems that a parent can solve. For example, a child might have seen a cobweb in the corner of her room. By carefully surveying the room with the child, and cleaning any areas that look suspicious, she might be reassured. On the other hand, perhaps a classmate has told a child that sometimes aliens visit children in the night and take them away. Explaining that there is no evidence for this might be sufficient to allay a child's fear. If you sensitively ask your child questions about why she is afraid, you might be able to elicit a reason that you might then be able to solve.

More often than not, the fears that children divulge to their parents cannot be allayed with reasoning and thoughtful explanations. The same is true with the more general fears that many children have, like fears of the dark, fears of monsters or fears of being kidnapped. You can try a reward approach with these children, but rewards associated with going to bed and staying in bed sometimes do not work quite as well with really fearful children. This is because their fear overrides their motivation to get the reward. That is, the painfulness of the fear trumps the pleasure that might accrue from getting the reward.

Bedtime fears can be so overwhelming that there are children whose fears are experienced as pure terror. The fear of staying alone for these terrified children can be so severe that it may as well be called a "bedtime phobia." Rewards alone rarely work for these children.

General Strategies that Help Reduce Some Bedtime Fears

Reassurance

Whether your child is feigning fear or whether she is truly terrified, it is always worthwhile to offer some reassurance. Empathically assuring her that she is truly safe and secure can be comforting to your child.

But, as noted, reassurance, and the incentive of a special treat, may not work when a child is more than a little fearful. The following are some additional ways to decrease your child's anxiety at bedtime if she is very fearful.

Elimination of Fear-Inducing Triggers

Many children watch scary television shows or play frightening video or computer games prior to going to bed. These activities may not be problematic when done in a common room in the house that is well lit, or in a room in which there are other people around. However, at bedtime, when faced with being alone in the dark, these shows and games may return to a child's mind and haunt her. Therefore, it may be worthwhile to have your child forgo these pleasures in the evening, if not throughout the day.

Consistent Bedtime Routines

Creating a consistent and enjoyable bedtime routine can help reduce your child's fears. Consistent routines are soothing, and most of us tend to deal better with the trials and tribulations of life when there is consistency, predictability and stability. With a consistent routine, especially one in which the last step is a pleasurable one, your child will become accustomed to the fact that each step of the routine signals that the next step is about to occur, and, by the end, she may be relaxed and comfortable enough to forget her fears and fall asleep.

A consistent and enjoyable bedtime routine often includes some time to wind down, followed by a bath, a change into pajamas, tooth brushing, a story, and then hugs and kisses goodnight. You may find it interesting to know that there has been research done that has shown that bedtime routines alone can be very effective in improving a young child's sleep.

Company

Many children derive comfort from having something special in their bedroom to keep them company at night. This could be a treasured stuffed animal, or a small pet, such as a little turtle or a goldfish. Therefore, you might consider giving your child one or more of these items to help reduce her fears.

Explanations

Offering explanations about the nighttime noises that frighten your child can help to reduce bedtime fears. These might include sounds like that of the house settling or of the heating system going on and shutting off.

Practice

Practicing exposure to bedtime experiences during the light of day can be helpful in the campaign against bedtime fears. You might want to have your child spend time alone in her bedroom during the day and then again at dusk. This strategy can be enhanced by simulating bedtime, such as by turning off the lights and pulling the window shades shut.

Relaxation Techniques

Teaching your child relaxation strategies can assist in reducing fears. It is hard for a child to feel tense and anxious when her body is relaxed. One type of relaxation technique is called *progressive muscle relaxation*. This program entails progressively tensing and relaxing different muscle groups, focusing on the experience of gradual relaxation that occurs when the muscles are relaxed. Another strategy involves listening to soothing CDs and audiotapes, such as those involving guided imagery (wherein the voice on the CD or tape describes the lush, sensory experiences that characterize a lovely, natural setting, like a park) and those involving nature sounds, such as the soothing sounds of rain or the ocean.

General Strategies Don't Always Work With Some Bedtime Fears

The strategies described above help many frightened children, but they usually will not do the trick when a child is absolutely terrified or phobic. Few parental challenges are as perplexing and as upsetting as putting a phobic child to sleep in her own bed. The separation anxiety a phobic child experiences can feel virtually unbearable to her. Moreover, because reassurances and other strategies often do not work, most parents become exhausted and exasperated. Parental frustration can often give way to threats, and parental threats can send frightened children into tears and tantrums. All too often, parents caught up in this situation give in and let their child fall asleep with them.

CO-SLEEPING

Incidentally, there are some parents who do not mind permitting their frightened child to sleep in the parental bed. Indeed, there are some parents who advocate having the family sleep together in one bed. However, it is one thing to believe in the family bed as a matter of principle, and it is another to resort to the family bed out of desperation.

Interventions to Help with Serious Bedtime Fears

Exposure

While reassurance and coping strategies can be helpful for mild to moderate fears of all sorts, they are often not sufficient for intense fears and phobias, bedtime phobias included. What usually does work, however, is a strategy involving exposure.

Exposure strategies, technically called "real-life desensitization" or "exposure therapy," involve exposing the frightened individual to the object of their fear. In the case of bedtime fears, the object of the fear is being alone in the bed at bedtime. Thus exposure for bedtime fears involves having the child spend time alone in her bed at bedtime. Exposure can be introduced suddenly or gradually. In the case of bedtime fears, this means either having the child spend the entire bedtime alone in her bed (sudden exposure) or having the child spend gradually increasing amounts of time alone in her bed (gradual exposure.)

How Exposure Programs Can Help Children with Bedtime Resistance

In the case of children with bedtime fears, exposure strategies teach the child that when she stays alone in her room, nothing bad will happen.

Exposure strategies are helpful for bedtime resisters as well. Bedtime resisters aren't afraid to stay alone; they just don't want to. So the goal with a bedtime resister is not to teach the child that nothing bad will happen when he is alone, but rather that he can manage without getting his way. It teaches him that, despite his tears and tantrums, he can tolerate the frustration and aggravation of not getting his way, which would be to stay up with his parents for as long as he would like.

Flooding and Implosion

The technical terms for exposure strategies that involve sudden exposure to the feared situation are "implosion" and "flooding." These are fancy terms that refer to a strategy involving having the frightened person be exposed, in full force, and without let-up, to the feared object. In the case of bedtime fears, this sort of exposure strategy would involve having the child stay in her room alone, and be left to cry it out until she eventually falls asleep.

Constant exposure to a feared situation usually leads to "habituation," the experience of becoming so used to the unpleasant sensation that it no longer feels particularly uncomfortable. Picture being at a swimming pool and diving into the water. People usually feel uncomfortably chilly at first. But with time, the body gets used to the cold water until eventually, the body feels comfortable. In the case of bedtime fears, repeated and prolonged exposure to being alone in the bedroom results in the child getting used to the experience. Over time, meaning over a period of successive nights, the child sees that she has managed to live through her fears. She sees that nothing bad happened. She becomes used to the experience of being alone so that she is no longer afraid.

Gradual Exposure

Because abrupt and prolonged exposure can be quite uncomfortable at first, both for the frightened individual as well as for those around her, many exposure therapies involve gradual exposure, in which the individual is gradually exposed to the feared object. In the case of bedtime fears, the child is gradually exposed to longer and longer periods of time alone in her bedroom. Gradual exposure can be achieved in several ways. However, the key to all gradual exposure programs remains the same: gradual exposure to the feared situation.

Shorter and Shorter Periods of Time at the Child's Bedside

One method of gradual exposure involves having the parent spend shorter and shorter periods of time at the child's bedside at bedtime. The first night could involve perhaps 15 minutes of bedside pleasantries (chit-chat, hugs, kisses and "goodnight,") once the bedtime routine is finished; followed the second night by 10 minutes of pleasantries after the established bedtime routine, followed the third night by 5 minutes of pleasantries after the established bedtime routine, followed on the last night by a mere hug, kiss and "nighty night" after the bedtime routine.

These time limits are not written in stone, of course. You could start with 15 minutes the first night, followed by 14 minutes the next night, 13 minutes the third night, and so forth, until your child is able to tolerate the ultimate "nighty-night," with no other pleasantries at all. Whatever works for you and your child.

Larger and Larger Amounts of Distance from the Child's Bedside

Another technique involves a variation on this theme. Instead of spending shorter and shorter periods of time at the child's bedside, the parent could sit larger and larger distances from the child's bed. You can start the first night by sitting in a chair at your child's bedside during the period of pleasantries. The next night you could perform the bedtime pleasantries six inches from your child's bedside. The subsequent night could involve sitting with your child a foot from her bedside and so on, until you are sitting outside the doorway and even in the hall.

Use Whatever Program Works

You need not utilize either of the programs that have just been described, or the procedure that follows; just make sure that you pick a procedure that exposes your child to longer and longer periods of time on her own in her room on a consistent basis.

And with whatever program you use, it is important to not require your child to fall asleep, just require her to stay alone. Your child can make herself stay in her own room, but she cannot *will* herself to sleep any more than you can *will* yourself to sleep. Her brain will determine when she enters a sleep state. Keep in mind, though, that no one stays awake forever; eventually, she will fall asleep.

~

All of these programs essentially involve leaving your child on her own for longer and longer periods of time. In time, she will realize that she can tolerate staying alone in her room. She comes to this realization because she sees that, indeed, she is staying alone in her room. She is being desensitized to staying alone through the actual process of staying alone. She becomes less and less sensitive about it until finally, she does not mind staying alone at all. Voila, you have a child who can fall asleep by herself.

Middle of the Night Wakings

Some children don't seem to have trouble at bedtime, but, instead, seem to only have problems in the middle of the night. They get up, in the middle of the night, and either call for their parents, or go into their parents' bedroom, even into their parents' bed.

The Regular Sleep Cycle

Falling asleep is one thing; staying asleep is another. All of us, children and adults alike, rise out of one sleep cycle before entering the next, multiple times during the night. Few of us are aware of these brief awakenings because we automatically return to sleep. What makes it so easy to return to sleep is that most of us have positive sleep associations.

Sleep Associations

Sleep associations are the objects in your room and your child's room that are present at bedtime, and become associated with the experience of falling asleep. These ordinarily include people and things. For you, this might mean your partner. For your child this might include a parent and perhaps a pet, like her pet gerbil. The objects in the child's room become part of the cue that triggers for her the sense of security and serenity that lulls her into sleep.

A positive sleep association helps your child fall asleep on her own. For example, if having a stuffed animal in the bed is part of the bedtime ritual, then, when she rouses in the middle of the night, however briefly, having the stuffed animal present helps her feel comfortable enough to fall back to sleep on her own.

A negative sleep association is something that can create a problem when your child tries to fall asleep on her own. For example, if a child is used to having a parent sit with him while he falls asleep, then that parent becomes a sleep association. The parent being there is associated with the experience of falling asleep. But if he wakes in the middle of the night and the parent is not there (because the parent is now sleeping in her own bedroom,) then he will have difficulty falling back to sleep because his sleep association (the parent) is not there.

The fact that the parent is there at bedtime makes the parent a sleep association, but the fact that the parent will not be there when the child arouses in the middle of the night makes the parent a negative sleep association.

The child has a sleep association that, instead of doing something positive, like facilitating sleep, does something negative, like interfering with sleep. It interferes with sleep because, as a result of not always being present in the child's bedroom, it creates the possibility for the child's becoming alarmed when he wakes in the middle of the night. When the parent is in his own bedroom, then he will not be present in his child's bedroom. But if his child has gotten used to his presence at bedtime then his absence is not part of what helps the child to comfortably fall back asleep in the middle of the night. In order for the parental sleep association to be present, the child needs to call for the parent to return, or get out of bed and go into the parent's bedroom to be with him. The child needs to be with the parent in order to have his sleep association reinstated. And the child will only be able to fall back to sleep comfortably with the parent (his sleep association) present.

Children who awaken in the middle of the night and do not fall right back to sleep are often children who have gotten used to having a parent stay with them at bedtime until they are either very sleepy or until they have actually fallen asleep. When the child awakes in the middle of the night, the absence of the parent is experienced as frightening because being without the parent has not been a part of bedtime and the onset of sleep.

When your child falls asleep all by himself at bedtime, his sleep associations do not include your presence. They do not include the presence of anything, that, if absent, will make it difficult for the child to fall back asleep when he awakens. As a result, his nighttime awakenings will be accompanied only by positive sleep associations, and he will be able to return to sleep on his own. He will have become accustomed to falling asleep by himself, and, upon awakening in the middle of the night, he will be able to fall right back to sleep.

Therefore, if your child is waking in the middle of the night and anxiously seeking you out, then the same exposure strategies that help children with bedtime fears will also help. Try the strategies that have been discussed so that your child can feel comfortable being in his own bed, all alone, at any point during bedtime and sleep time.

The Technique Used in the Children's Story

Longer and Longer Periods of Time Away from the Child's Bedroom

The procedure depicted in the children's story associated with this book, *Goodbye to Bedtime Fears,* is one of the more popular approaches to the problem, and it has been the subject of a considerable amount of research. Its technical labels are "graduated extinction" and "graduated ignoring." It involves leaving the child alone in her bedroom for longer and longer periods of time. At first, the parent leaves for just a moment or two, and then comes back. Subsequently, the parent leaves the child alone for a slightly longer period of time, and then, just as before, returns. Once again, the child becomes desensitized by seeing that she is capable of staying alone because, in fact, she *is* staying alone.

Advance Preparation

Bedtime desensitization procedures can work; and they can work within days; but they require persistence and determination, often in the face of tearful resistance from your child. Children sometimes cry during the first attempts to leave them; and it can be heart-wrenching to hear your child cry. Therefore, it is extremely helpful if you prepare, in advance, for your child's resistance. The more you are prepared, the easier it will be to follow through on the desensitization.

Address Your Child's Bedroom Fears

Some children are not only fearful of being in their room at bedtime, they are fearful staying in their room, alone, *anytime*, day *and* night. If this is the case for your child, then a gradual exposure treatment of her bedtime phobia will be all that much more difficult, because you will be trying to tackle bedroom and bedtime phobias at the same time. You can increase the likelihood of successfully conquering her bedtime fears by first helping her to become comfortable with staying in her room alone during the day.

As described earlier, you might be able to accomplish this with the incentive of a reward. For example, you may be able to motivate her to stay alone in her room by enticing her with a variety of small treats that she can earn if she stays in her room, alone, for longer and longer periods of time.

You may also want to try a creative approach, such as incorporating the experience of staying in her room alone into a game. The game of hide-and-go-seek works well for this venture. The game involves having one person remain in the child's room alone, counting to 30 aloud, while the other player finds a place in the house to hide. After the count of 30, the player who was initially in the child's bedroom then ventures out of the room to find their hidden opponent. You might want to start the game by first having *you* remain in her room, counting to 30, while *she* hides somewhere in the house; followed by having *her* remain in her room, counting to 30, while *you* hide somewhere in the house. You can follow this by playing the game with all the lights off in the house; followed, finally, by playing the game in the evening with, and then without, the lights on.

Create a Bedtime Routine

Before launching your exposure program, you should devise a bedtime routine. As described before, this may include some time to wind down, followed by a bath, a change into sleep attire, tooth brushing, stories and a hug and kiss goodnight. The key to a good bedtime routine is to come up with something that is soothing, pleasurable and has qualities that enable it to be performed with consistency.

Prepare Your Child for the Program

Now that you've created the routine, review it with your child, and prepare her for the fact that eventually you will be separating from her at the end of it.

Read *Goodbye to Bedtime Fears* with Your Child

You will probably want to read to your child the children's story about Emily, the little girl who, like your child, is afraid to sleep in her own bed. (Please read the story to yourself before you read it to your child. You will want to make sure that you feel it is appropriate for your child. Reading it in advance by yourself will also prepare you for your child's reactions to the story.)

In *Goodbye to Bedtime Fears*, Emily is able to learn how to fall asleep while alone in her bedroom. Most people enjoy hearing stories about others who have overcome obstacles like their own. Your child will probably find it inspirational and motivating to learn that another child, Emily, has conquered the same fear that *she* is trying to conquer.

You may want to ask your child questions about the story and questions about her thoughts and feelings about your plan to desensitize her from her fear of being alone at night. Her answers to your questions may help you to troubleshoot any problems with your plans. For example, she may tell you that she will feel better if you make sure to place her favorite stuffed animal on her bed. Or, perhaps she will tell you that she will feel better if you sing her favorite lullaby before you leave her room.

Discuss Coping Techniques with Your Child

You may also want to discuss coping techniques with your child. For example, you may want to teach her different ways to relax her body by showing her how to take slow, deep breaths to help her to relax. You might want to help her imagine comforting and relaxing pictures in her mind (such as an image of you sitting on a rocker next to her bed, smiling down at her.) You might also want to teach her different positive statements that she can repeat to herself over and over to make herself feel more confident in the face of her separation fears, like "I'm completely safe, there's nothing to fear."

Prepare *Yourself* for the Program

Finally, you should thoroughly prepare yourself for the difficulties that *you* might encounter while performing the desensitization procedure. The strategy requires that when you leave your child's room, your child must stay in her room, preferably in her bed. Since your child has been afraid to stay alone in her room, she may not stay there the first time you leave. Your child may bolt out of her bed and try to leave her room the first time you try to leave. If your child does this, then you may want to stand at her doorway, and calmly tell her that she has to get back into her bed, and that you will not come over to her bed to comfort her until she does so. You may even want to close her door, and tell her that you will not open it until she returns to her bed. How will you know whether or not she has returned to her bed? Well, you will not know for sure without checking; so you can open up her door a crack from time to time to check, making sure to close it quickly if you see that she has not returned to her bed. Make sure to close the door carefully, just in case little fingers are too close to the door frame.

Prepare for the Possibility that Your Child May Cry

Listening to a child cry can be very hard to take, especially if it is *your* child. It may happen, so *please prepare* for it. It helps to keep in mind that you are asking your child to stay alone in her bedroom, not in a lion's den. You are asking her to do something that you feel is safe. If you do not feel that it is safe for your child to stay in her room alone, then you must figure out a way to make it safe. You cannot embark on an exposure program until your child really *is* safe.

Also, once you have made certain that your child is safe in her room, you still should not try such a program until *you* feel really comfortable that your child is safe. If you do not feel she is safe, you are not going to have the heart to make her stay in her room when *she* is fearful that she is unsafe.

Regarding safety, if you think about it, it is practically impossible to 100% safety-proof your home, even if you paid bodyguards to surround your house 24/7. But just like with many other things in life (for example, driving a car or crossing the street,) there is risk when we go to bed at night. Risk is a part of life. And so, like with all the other risks that you take, you do your very best to get used to the teeny tiny chance of something going awry when you are in your bed at night. Likewise, you want to help your child be able to do the same.

Remember, too, that you are performing the exposure program at night, and your child is probably tired. Tired children can often be irritable and tearful. So, if your child is crying, keep in mind that her tears may be the tears of exhaustion and not rage. Do not be deterred if your child becomes furious, and tells you that she is very mad at you when you insist that she stay alone in her room. You are exposing your child to anxiety, and anxiety hurts. As a result, your child may be angry with you for inflicting discomfort; but keep in mind that you are doing it for her own good. Part of being a parent is exposing your child to discomfort; like polio vaccination, homework, the taste of broccoli. So, if you do not believe in the family bed, and, instead, subscribe to the value system of having a child be independent at night, then exposing your child to the discomfort of being alone in her own bed is a fact of her life. Gradual exposure to anxiety-provoking situations is what ultimately makes the situations less anxiety-provoking— helping your child be less anxious in a place that she should not be anxious: her own room—and that is what you need to accomplish.

This procedure will go more smoothly if you think about it in these benign terms rather than if you believe that you are being cruel. If you are not sure about all this, you may want to consult with your pediatrician or a mental health professional for reassurance and advice.

It may surprise you that research done on this procedure has not shown that children suffer ill-effects from it. In fact, much of the research has demonstrated that, once the procedure is completed, children tend to be better-adjusted than they were before the procedure was undertaken. The parent-child relationship tends to improve as well.

You may find this hard to believe when your child is crying her head off. But if you are like most parents who have gotten to the point where they need to resort to a gradual exposure strategy, then you have probably had many angry and tearful nights, with you losing your temper and your child crying in response. All that tension disappears when the gradual exposure program is successfully completed. So it follows that, after the program is completed, your child will be better adjusted and your relationship with your child will improve.

The Procedure Takes Time, But It Can Work

The nightly procedure takes some time because you are not done until your child is quietly tolerating staying in her room on her own. But remember, human beings, children included, cannot stay awake and cry forever. As you alternately leave and then return to her room, it will be getting later in the evening. As the evening wears on, your child will be getting drowsier, even more so if she has worn herself out with crying.

Eventually, during one of the intervals when you are away from her, she will fall asleep. When she awakens, either in the middle of the night, or the next morning, she will awaken to the realization that she fell asleep all by herself. With time, she will come to realize that she *can* stay alone. By the way, if she awakens in the middle of the night and comes into your room, you really must return her to her bed and continue the procedure until she is, again, able to calmly stay in her room.

Because this nightly procedure can be emotionally draining, and because it occurs late in the evening, you may begin to feel unbearably tired. If your child has not demonstrated that she can handle being alone without being frightened, then please don't succumb to your exhaustion by retiring to your bedroom to go to sleep before your child is asleep. If she is still anxiously awake during one of the intervals, waiting for your return, and she finds that you've gone into your bedroom to go to sleep for the night, she'll probably become extremely upset. You're doing the program of gradual exposure because she is afraid to stay alone in her room. It involves trusting that you're awake and will keep her safe until she falls asleep. If she feels that she can't trust you, which she will feel if she's been presuming that you'll eventually return within a certain amount of time and you don't, then she may be even more frightened the next time you attempt this procedure, and it will take that much longer to calm her down.

Eventually, once she has become accustomed to staying alone in her bedroom without fear, and it's clear that she won't be expecting or wanting you to come in and check on her, then, if you'd like, you can retire to your room and go to sleep. Keep in mind, though, that some children become frightened if they feel that they're the only ones awake in the home. But if you sense that your child is no longer frightened by this, then, if you feel comfortable doing so, you can retire. You won't need to wait until she is asleep if she is staying calm and quiet in her own room waiting for sleep to overcome her. But, until she has demonstrated that she is no longer frightened to stay in her room by herself, you should stay awake, so as to provide reassurance that you will be alert, and ready and able to take on any of her imagined threats to her safety.

Be Consistent

You can see that the nightly process of training your child to stay alone in her room at night can take many minutes, or even many hours. Therefore, it is very important that you only begin the procedure when you are certain that you will have the patience and energy to persist and prevail, and that you will be able to tolerate the possibility that your child may be very tired in the morning and may not fare well at school. If you attempt the procedure and then cave in when your child begins to cry, or when it gets late and you are absolutely exhausted, then you will only make matters worse. Your child will learn that her tears or your exhaustion can persuade you into letting her fall asleep with you, rather than on her own. She will learn that if she cries at least as hard or as long the next time you try this process, then you will give in again and let her stay with you.

If the procedure becomes too upsetting and difficult for you or your child, then remember this: you can opt for a co-sleeping arrangement. You do not *need* to make your child sleep alone. But choose one or the other; do not go back and forth. When you let her sleep with you, your behavior implies that sleeping with you is acceptable. Then, when you require her to sleep alone the next night, your behavior will seem unfair and cruel. You will be withholding from her something that she desperately wants; something that only yesterday you felt was okay to do. She will think that you are being mean. She will think that if you thought it was okay last night, then by not letting her sleep with you tonight you must not care about her feelings. Furthermore, having let her sleep with you last night, she will feel motivated to protest all that much more tonight, in the hope that, like last night, you will change your mind. So, keep in mind that if you go back and forth, you will make everyone more miserable.

Recommended Wait Times

Many professionals, including psychologists and pediatricians, have written articles and books about this bedtime procedure. Some recommend an elaborate system of wait times that involves staying away for five minutes the first time on the first night, and then gradually lengthening the time you stay away until the child is asleep. What is recommended then, is that, on the first night, you require your child to stay alone for five minutes before checking in on her. Checking in should only last about 30 seconds. If she continues to cry or fuss after you have checked in, then it is recommended that you leave the room again, for an *extra* five minutes (meaning ten minutes in total) before checking in for the second time. If she is still crying when you check in for the third time, then you are to leave the room again, adding five minutes (now for a total of fifteen minutes.) After your third visit you are to only make brief check-ins every fifteen minutes until your child is no longer crying, at which point no more checks are to be made.

On each subsequent night of the procedure, all the check-ins are to be lengthened by five minutes. This means that, on the second night of the procedure, your child is left alone in her room for ten minutes before the first check-in, fifteen minutes before the second check-in and 20 minutes before the third check-in and before all subsequent check-ins. On the third night, the first departure should last fifteen minutes, with five minutes added to each subsequent check-in, and so forth, as before, throughout the evening.

Not every professional recommends this schedule of wait times. Some recommend staying away for a few minutes at a time, while others recommend staying away for 30 seconds. The lengths of the wait time are not cut in stone. If you find it impossible to listen to your child crying for even 30 seconds, then you can experiment with even shorter times to begin the process. For example, you may want to try a first wait on the first night of only three seconds. You can listen to your child cry for three seconds, can't you? That's just "one, one thousand; two, one thousand; three, one thousand."

It isn't always necessary to use specific time intervals in order to teach your child that she is able to stay alone in her room at night. Instead of a specific amount of time, you can use specific activities that require you to leave his room. Should you try this approach, you'll want to start, at first, with a very short activity; for example, going into another room to turn off a light, or going into the kitchen to turn on the dishwasher. You can graduate from this brief wait period to one that is longer, such as leaving to put the wash in the washing machine or to fold the clothes that you've taken out of the dryer. Of course, with this approach it is important that your child is old enough to understand the relative time involved in your departure. You will want him to understand that going into the kitchen to turn on the dishwasher only takes a few seconds, as opposed to folding the clothes, which may take a few minutes. With whatever procedure you use, make sure to behave in a reliable and trustworthy manner. Your child is learning to ease her anxiety about staying alone. You do not want to introduce into the situation anxiety about whether or not he can trust that you will return within a reasonable period of time.

Remember that if you tamper with the wait times, you should try to lengthen each wait time a bit, to gradually give your child a chance to learn to soothe herself and to show her that she can handle longer and longer intervals of being alone. You must not tamper with the wait times in such a way as to give her the impression that if she cries then you will come in sooner. This defeats the whole purpose of this exercise, and, once again, teaches her that her tears can persuade you to cave in. The goal is for her to learn that, indeed, she *can* stay alone at bedtime; so you need to give her time alone, tears or no tears, so that she can see that she really *can* do it. If you go in to rescue her too soon, you are depriving her of a chance to be successful.

Recommended Check-in Behavior

Your check-ins should be very brief, seconds if you feel you and your child can handle it, preferably no longer than a minute. And while you can go over to her and offer a comment of reassurance, it is important to not engage in any lengthy conversation. This is not the time to discuss the importance of his learning how to handle being alone in his room. Your checking in is simply for the purpose of demonstrating to him that you are still present, and reassuring yourself that everything is okay. If you can achieve this by merely standing at his door for a second or two, all the better.

Other Ways to Make the Procedure More Tolerable

There are other things you can do to make this process easier for yourself and your child. For example, if you find that you have to close the door because your child is anxiously trying to get out of her bedroom to be with you, then you can stand right outside the door and offer comforting remarks, which will remind her that she is not really alone in the home. But remember, try not to talk too much, or she will begin to need your talking to help her be alone, which, in effect, is not really being alone.

If you have a partner in your home, you might want to alternate the task of leaving and returning to your child's room with that person, so that you need not subject yourself to too much discomfort and exhaustion as you listen to your child fuss.

Steps to the Technique Used in the Children's Story

Hopefully, these preparations have gotten you ready to try the procedure. Now, here are the steps:

1. Perform the bedtime routine.

2. Leave your child's room. If your child tries to leave her room, then block her from doing so (with your body, with a door, with a gate, etc.)

3. Return to your child's room and check on her. Comfort her for a few seconds, if necessary.

4. Leave your child's room again. This time, stay out of her room for a somewhat longer period than you did last time.

5. Perform steps 3 and 4 repeatedly until your child is calmly staying in her room, preferably in her bed.

6. You are done for the night. Consider giving your child a reward the next morning to underscore your pride in her success (and to motivate her for the next night.) In fact, you may want to give her a small reward each time she manages to get through a wait period.

7. Repeat steps 1 through 6 each successive night until you have a child who does not fuss when you leave her alone at bedtime.

This program is not complicated, but it can be emotionally and physically draining.

Should you be unable to resolve your child's bedtime fears after having read about the issues and strategies, and having perhaps tried the techniques offered in this book, then you may want to consult with a professional, such as your pediatrician or a therapist specializing in work with children.

Resources to Help you get your ZZZZs

There are other fine books available that provide details regarding this procedure and the related techniques, such as relaxation and breathing exercises, guided imagery and positive self-talk. Below is a list of some of these. Also included are some children's books that can serve as very good bedtime stories for children who are anxious and resistant about going to bed. If, after all of this, you still feel that you simply cannot get your child over her fears enough to stay on her own at bedtime, then you may want to consult with your pediatrician, or with a mental health professional. Good luck!

Books for Parents

Solve Your Child's Sleep Problems. Richard Ferber. New York: Simon Schuster, Inc., 1985.

Good Night, Sweet Dreams, I Love You: Now Get Into Bed and Go to Sleep! Patrick Friman. Boys Town, Nebraska: Boys Town Press, 2005.

Monsters Under the Bed and Other Childhood Fears. Stephen W. Garber, Marianne Daniels Garber, and Robyn Freedman Spizman. New York: Villard Books, a division of Random House, Inc., 1993.

Break the Co-Sleeping Habit: How to Set Bedtime Boundaries – and Raise a Secure, Happy, Well-Adjusted Child. Valerie Levine. Avon, Massachusetts: Adams Media, 2009.

Sleeping Through the Night. Jodi Mindell. New York: HarperCollins. 1997.

Take Charge of Your Child's Sleep. Judy Owens, M.D. and Jodi Mindell, Ph.D. New York: Marlowe and Company, 2005.

The No-Cry Sleep Solution for Toddlers and Preschoolers. Elizabeth Pantley. New York: McGraw-Hill, 2005.

Baby and Toddler Sleep Program. John Pearce, M.D. with Jane Bidder. Tuscon, Arizona: Fisher Books, LLC, 1999.

Good Night, Sleep Tight. Kim West with Joanne Kenen. CDC Books, 2006.

Books for Children

Goodnight, Sleep Tight, Little Bunnies. Dawn Apperley. New York: Scholastic, Inc. 2002.

Close Your Eyes. Kate Banks. New York: Farrar, Straus & Giroux, 2002.

Bedtime for Little Bears. David Bedford. Good Books, 2008.

Oliver Who Would Not Sleep. Mara Bergman. New York: Arthur A. Levine Books, 2007.

The Going to Bed Book. Sandra Boynton. New York: Little Simon, 1982.

Pajama Time! Sandra Boyton. New York: Workman Publishing Company, 2000.

Goodnight Moon. Margaret Wise Brown. Harper Festival, 1991.

I Love You, Sleepyhead. Claire Freedman. Good Books, 2007.

Time For Bed. Mem Fox. New York: Harcourt, Inc., 1993.

Kiss Good Night. Amy Hest. Cambridge, Massachusetts: Candlewick Press, 2001.

Tigers Love to Say Goodnight. Sue Mongredien. London, England: Orchard Books, 2008.

The Sleep Ponies. Gudrun Ongman. Mindcastle Books, 2000.

The Sleep Fairy. Janie Peterson. Omaha, Nebraska: Behave'n Kids Press, Inc., 2003.

Good Night, Good Knight. Shelley Moore Thomas. New York: Puffin Press, 2001.

The Noisy Way to Bed. Ian Whybrow. New York: Arthur A. Levine Books, 2004.

My Goodnight Book. Eloise Wilkin. Golden Books, 1995.

Don't Let the Pigeon Stay Up Too Late. Mo Willems. New York: Hyperion Books for Children, 2006.

Sleepyhead. Karma Wilson. Simon and Schuster, 2006.

The Goodnight Book for moms and little ones. Edited by Alice Wong and Lean Taberi. New York: Welcome Books, an imprint of Welcome Enterprises, Inc., 2005.

How do Dinosaurs Say Goodnight? Jane Yolen. New York: The Blue Sky Press, 2000.